# Spooky Museums

## by Joyce Markovics

Consultant: Ryan Lintelman
Curator, National Museum of American History
Washington, DC

BEARPORT
PUBLISHING

New York, New York

## Credits

Cover, © Kim Jones; 6, © The Warren's Occult Museum; 7, © The Warren's Occult Museum; 8, © Droopydogajna/Dreamstime; 9T, © Everett Historical/Shutterstock; 9B, © Cleveland Museum of Art; 10, © Jennifer Boyer/CC BY-ND 4.0; 11L, © Bernard McManus/CC BY 4.0; 11R, © Schwerdf/CC BY 4.0; 12, © Alan Jeffery/Shutterstock; 13T, © somewhere else/Alamy; 13B, © Mary Evans Picture Library Ltd/AGE Fotostock; 14, © Philip Scalia/Alamy; 15T, © sNIke/Shutterstock and © revers/Shutterstock; 15B, © W. Metzen/ClassicStock; 16, © russellkord.com/AGE Fotostock; 17, © GUIZIOU Franck/Hemis/AGE Fotostock; 18, © Amaury Laporte/CC BY-NC 4.0; 19L, Public Domain; 19R, © John Mosbaugh/CC BY-4.0; 20, © Scott Beale/CC BY-NC-ND 4.0; 21L, © Catmando/Shutterstock; 21R, © RichVintage/iStock; 22, © Chemical Engineer/Public Domain; 23, © Thackray Medical Museum; 24, © Liesl Vandepaepeliere/Shutterstock; 25, © The Print Collector/Alamy and © Steve Collender/Shutterstock; 26, © Tony Baggett/Shutterstock; 27, © Wojtek Buss/AGE Fotostock; 31, © saiko3p/Shutterstock.

Publisher: Kenn Goin
Senior Editor: Joyce Tavolacci
Creative Director: Spencer Brinker
Design: Dawn Beard Creative
Cover: Kim Jones
Photo Researcher: Picture Perfect Professionals, LLC

Library of Congress Cataloging-in-Publication Data in process at time of publication (2018)
Library of Congress Control Number: 2017045551
ISBN-13: 978-1-68402-437-7 (library binding)

For more information, write to Bearport Publishing Company, Inc., 45 West 21st Street, Suite 3B, New York, New York 10010. Printed in the United States of America.

10 9 8 7 6 5 4 3 2 1

# Contents

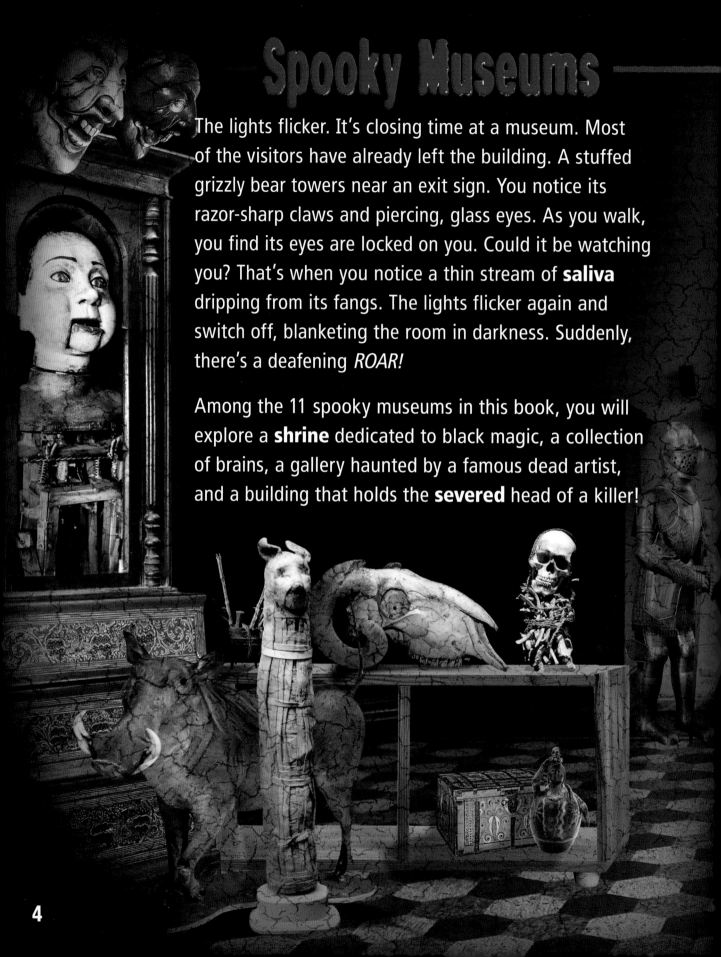

# Spooky Museums

The lights flicker. It's closing time at a museum. Most of the visitors have already left the building. A stuffed grizzly bear towers near an exit sign. You notice its razor-sharp claws and piercing, glass eyes. As you walk, you find its eyes are locked on you. Could it be watching you? That's when you notice a thin stream of **saliva** dripping from its fangs. The lights flicker again and switch off, blanketing the room in darkness. Suddenly, there's a deafening *ROAR!*

Among the 11 spooky museums in this book, you will explore a **shrine** dedicated to black magic, a collection of brains, a gallery haunted by a famous dead artist, and a building that holds the **severed** head of a killer!

# The Devil Doll

## Warrens' Occult Museum, Monroe, Connecticut

This small museum is truly the stuff of nightmares. Among its haunted treasures are children's tombstones and a mirror that can **summon** spirits. The centerpiece of the collection is a wicked doll.

Warrens'
Occult Museum

Opened in 1952, this museum contains the personal collection of Ed and Lorraine Warren. For decades, the Warrens worked as ghost hunters. During that time, they investigated more than 10,000 spooky cases and collected any creepy items they found. The Warrens housed their collection in the basement of their own home in Connecticut.

One of the Warrens' most prized objects is a grinning doll called Annabelle. The rag doll once belonged to a woman named Donna, who claimed it would move mysteriously around her apartment. It also left creepy handwritten messages, including a note that read, "Help us." One night, the rag doll slowly glided up the leg of one of Donna's friends as he was fast asleep. Then it latched onto his throat and tried to strangle him! Frightened for her life, Donna contacted the Warrens. They were certain that the spirit of a dead girl named Annabelle Higgins **possessed** the doll. The couple took the doll and placed it in their museum.

Visitors to the Warrens' Occult Museum can view Annabelle in a glass box. A sign warns people to absolutely not open the case . . . or else.

The Warrens' museum also includes a coffin supposedly used by a vampire.

The Warrens and Annabelle, the doll

# Dead Ringer

## Cleveland Museum of Art, Cleveland, Ohio

Within this historic museum are priceless works of art by famous artists such as Pablo Picasso and Claude Monet. Visitors enjoy gazing at the masterpieces. Who—or what—else might be looking at the art? The answer will send shivers down your spine.

Cleveland Museum of Art

French artist Claude Monet died in 1926. He is most famous for his colorful, airy paintings, as well as his bushy white beard. In 2015, workers were putting the finishing touches on a new exhibit of Monet's art at the Cleveland Museum of Art when, suddenly, a museum staff member noticed something strange on a balcony above the gallery. "This man resembling Claude Monet was . . . peering down into the lower lobby," said the worker. He immediately snapped a photo to show others what he had seen.

Claude Monet

Many agree that the creepy person in the photo is a **dead ringer** for the artist Claude Monet. "What are the chances someone looks like that and happens to be at the museum the day we are finishing installation?" said another museum worker. Could it be Monet's ghost?

The actual photo taken by a museum worker

A former Cleveland Museum of Art director has also been spotted wandering in the oldest part of the building. He died in 1978.

# A Chilling Collection

## Museum of Icelandic Sorcery and Witchcraft, Hólmavík, Iceland

In a small town in Iceland sits a plain, wooden building. No one would ever guess that this place is a shrine to **sorcery**. The museum offers a glimpse into Iceland's past . . . and black magic.

Museum of Icelandic Sorcery and Witchcraft

Galdrasýning á Ströndum
Museum of Sorcery & Witchcraft

First opened in 2000, the museum includes animal skulls, books of magic, and other odd objects related to witchcraft. Many visitors are drawn to the museum's "necropants," which are trousers made from real human skin! Long ago, it was believed that necropants could make their owners rich.

According to **folklore**, to make the pants, a dead man was dug up from his grave and skinned from the waist down. Then a coin was placed inside the necropants. It was said that whoever put on the terrifying trousers would become very wealthy. However, this only happened after the dead man's skin **melded** to his own!

A display showing what actual necropants might have looked like

Some books of magic, called *grimoires*, explain how to create magical objects, perform spells, and summon demons.

A magical symbol called a stave used for making necropants

11

# The Spooky Staircase

## Queen's House, National Maritime Museum, Greenwich, England

Step inside this historic museum and former **royal** home to find the spiraling Tulip Stairs. This grand staircase has a flowery iron railing and twists all the way up to the top floor. Curiously, the staircase is a favorite spot for spirits.

Queen's House

In 1966, a visitor to the museum, the Reverend Ralph Hardy of British Columbia, snapped a picture of the elegant staircase. When he returned home and developed the film, he was shocked at what he saw. The photo revealed two **shrouded** figures pulling themselves up the railing of the stairs with their hands. What had Reverend Hardy captured in the picture? To this day, no one is quite sure.

The Tulip Stairs

The photo isn't the only evidence of ghostly goings-on in the museum. In 2002, a worker saw a figure wearing an old-fashioned gray dress. "I went very cold, and the hair on my arms and my neck stood on end," the worker said. Then the figure passed right through a wall. Mysterious footsteps and the sound of children chanting have also been heard in the stairwell.

Reverend Ralph Hardy's photo, which shows two ghostly figures

The Queen's House was built between 1616 and 1635. Previously used as a royal residence, it's now an art museum.

# Curious and Creepy

## Mütter Museum, Philadelphia, Pennsylvania

At the Mütter Museum, visitors enter a large room filled with hundreds of glass cases. When they look closer, they come face to face with **curiosities** beyond imagination.

Mütter
Museum

This museum got its name from Dr. Thomas Dent Mütter (1811–1859), a Philadelphia **surgeon**. He devoted his life to helping others—and to collecting some very unusual things. In addition to medical tools, Dr. Mütter collected human bones and **tumors** from his patients. In all, he acquired 1,700 odd items, with which he created a museum.

Today, more than 25,000 objects are housed at the Mütter Museum. Some of the most interesting pieces include **conjoined** twins and a book bound in human skin! One of the most amazing collections is made up of 2,374 objects that had been removed from people's throats and airways. These include coins, toys, and buttons. There is also a series of slides that displays actual slices of brain tissue. One of the tissue samples belongs to the famous scientist Albert Einstein!

The Mütter Museum first opened its doors to visitors in 1863.

# A Hideous History

**American Museum of Natural History, New York, New York**

This New York landmark is one of the largest natural history museums in the world. It holds 30 million **artifacts**. What secrets are hidden in this famous old stone building? See for yourself.

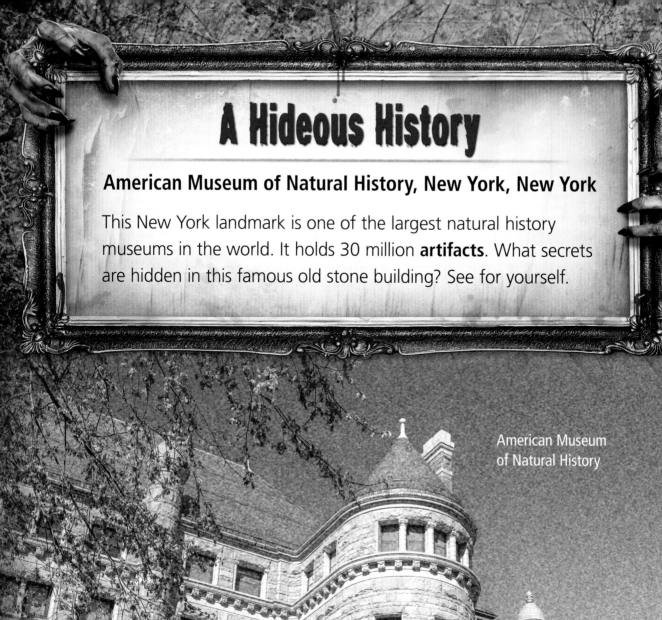

American Museum
of Natural History

The American Museum of Natural History is famous for its displays that feature creatures from around the world. "Sometimes you feel like the animals are watching you," says Frank Saunders, a night guard at the museum. For many visitors, the animals appear real. Why? It's probably because they were made using the fur, skin, teeth, and bones from animals that were once alive!

In another part of the museum, near a display of Native American artifacts, Saunders says he once heard chanting. Also, while looking at models of Native Americans, he thought he saw "veins **pulsating** and **tendons** moving."

If you want to see for yourself what's stirring at the museum, you can arrange to spend the night there. But it may be best to sleep with one eye open.

A stuffed tiger at the museum

The American Museum of Natural History was founded in 1869.

# Viewers, Beware!

## Museum of Death, Los Angeles, California

With a name that says it all, this museum doesn't shy away from death. Its collection of coffins and other **grisly** trinkets promises to make your skin crawl.

Museum of Death

The museum opened in 1995 in a building that used to be a **mortuary**. Its first exhibit was a collection of artwork made by murderers. From there, the museum's owners gathered personal items that belonged to **serial killers**, including letters and drawings. Over the years, the collection grew to include everything from body bags to bloody crime-scene photos.

One of the museum's most shocking pieces is a severed head. The head belonged to serial killer Henri Désiré Landru, who was born in Paris in 1869. Landru killed ten people between 1915 and 1919. After he killed them, he burned their bodies. In 1919, he was found guilty of the murders, and in 1922, he was beheaded in France. Although his body was buried, his head was preserved. Today, visitors to the museum can look into the eyes of a real-life monster.

Landru's severed head

The serial killer Henri Landru

In 2014, the Museum of Death opened a second location in New Orleans, Louisiana.

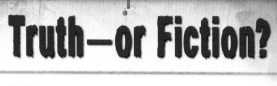

# Truth—or Fiction?

## International Cryptozoology Museum, Portland, Maine

Does Bigfoot really prowl **secluded** forests? Is the Loch Ness Monster real? The International Cryptozoology Museum might hold some clues. Visitors can look at the more than 10,000 items on display and then decide for themselves what's real and what's not.

International
Cryptozoology
Museum

MONSTERS
of MASSACHUSETTS

Loren Coleman is the museum's founder and a famous cryptozoologist. Cryptozoology is the study of creatures widely believed to exist only in legends. Over the years, Coleman has collected everything from photos of strange beasts to **casts** of huge footprints made by unknown animals. He's especially proud of the museum's hair and poop samples, which are said to belong to a Yeti.

In folklore, a Yeti is a large hairy creature that walks on two legs. Over the years, there have been many reports of Yeti sightings. In 1925, an explorer named N. A. Tombazi spotted a large creature near Zemu Glacier in the Himalaya Mountains. "Unquestionably, the figure in outline was exactly like a human being, walking upright," he said. "It showed up dark against the snow."

Coleman simply asks that museum visitors keep an open mind. He invites people to examine the objects and consider for themselves: Could there be undiscovered, weird creatures living in the world?

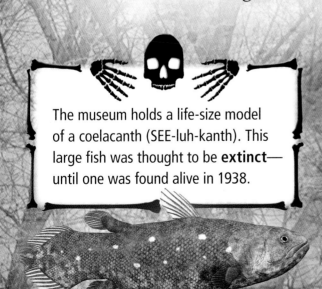

The museum holds a life-size model of a coelacanth (SEE-luh-kanth). This large fish was thought to be **extinct**—until one was found alive in 1938.

A photo of a supposed Yeti

# Cries and Dark Shadows

**Thackray Medical Museum, Leeds, West Yorkshire, England**

"Shhh . . . did you hear that?" It's best not to enter this museum at night. Despite its grand exterior, the building has a frightful past. It's a place where the dead are very much alive.

Thackray Medical Museum

The museum has large displays that show what life was like in the 1800s. One exhibit, "Pain, Pus, and Blood," describes surgery before **anesthesia**. Another display is devoted to the Yorkshire Witch, whose real name was Mary Bateman. Mary was a thief, who tricked people into believing she had magical powers. In 1806, she poisoned a woman after promising to help her. In 1809, Mary was **executed** for murder—and witchcraft. For years, her skeleton hung on display at the museum. After her death, strips of Mary's skin were dried and sold as magic charms.

In addition to taking in the spooky exhibits, museum visitors have also had creepy encounters. Some say they were grabbed by unseen hands. Reports of darting shadows and whimpering voices are also common. Is this museum creepy or cool? You be the judge.

The building that houses the museum opened in 1861 as the Leeds Union Workhouse, where very poor people lived and worked. Later, it was a hospital. In 1997, the building became the Thackray Medical Museum.

Box of medical tools from the 1800s

# The Bloody Butcher

## The Louvre, Paris, France

Each year, millions of people go to the Louvre in France to see its huge art collection. Yet the museum holds more than just priceless art. Once described as the most haunted place in Paris, the Louvre is for art lovers who aren't afraid of ghosts.

The Louvre museum

Parts of the Louvre date back to 1190, when it was used as a fortress and prison. In the late 1500s, it was also the site of the bloody St. Bartholomew's Day **Massacre**. The massacre began in 1572 after a series of killings involving French leaders. As many as 30,000 people were **slaughtered** in the streets.

It's no surprise that ghostly visitors linger at the museum. There have been sightings of old prison guards, as well as the Red Man of the Tuileries—a 16th-century murderer. His real name was John the Skinner, and he worked as a butcher. It's said that the Queen of France ordered him to kill her enemies. Then the queen decided to kill John by having his throat slashed. Before he died, John said, "I will be back." Since that time, a blood-soaked man has been spotted haunting the Louvre.

Some people believe the Louvre holds artworks painted with human blood!

A detail of a painting of the St. Bartholomew's Day Massacre

# The Cursed Coffin

## The British Museum, London, England

This museum houses one of the largest collections of ancient Egyptian artifacts in the world. One of the objects is a 3,500-year-old coffin that once held the mummy of a high **priestess**. Many believe the coffin is cursed.

The British Museum

The tale of the mummy's curse begins in 1865. At that time, an Englishman named Thomas D. Murray was visiting Egypt. There he purchased an ancient Egyptian coffin. A few days later, while Murray was hunting for ducks along the Nile River, he accidentally shot himself in the arm. Then two of Murray's servants who had helped move the coffin died.

Once back in London, Murray was visited by a **clairvoyant**, who warned him of the coffin's evil powers. Soon after, a photographer who had taken a picture of the coffin died suddenly. When the photo was developed, it captured a ghostly, terrifying face. In 1889, the coffin was brought to the British Museum. A worker who touched the case was struck down with a deadly illness. Then museum cleaning crews reported that they were overcome with terror any time they went near the mummy case. Is the coffin's curse real?

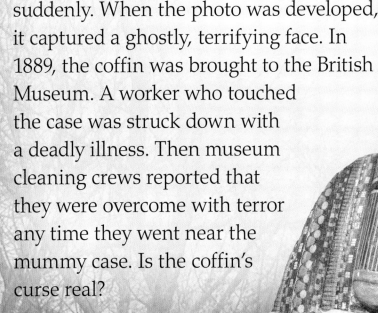

"Priestess, dead centuries ago, still **potent** to slay and **afflict**," read a 1904 newspaper. The headline referred to the ancient coffin Murray found.

# Spooky Museums

### Mütter Museum
**Philadelphia, Pennsylvania**

Stop off at a medical museum that's filled with curiosities.

### International Cryptozoology Museum
**Portland, Maine**

What's real and what's not at this museum—you be the judge.

### Museum of Death,
**Los Angeles, California**

This creepy collection will make your skin crawl.

### Warrens' Occult Museum
**Monroe, Connecticut**

Visit a spooky museum that holds a killer doll.

NORTH AMERICA

### Cleveland Museum of Art
**Cleveland, Ohio**

Get ready to meet an art-loving apparition.

### American Museum of Natural History
**New York, New York**

What secrets is this famous old museum hiding?

SOUTH AMERICA

*Atlantic Ocean*

*Pacific Ocean*

# Around the World

**Museum of Icelandic Sorcery and Witchcraft**
**Hólmavík, Iceland**

Take a look at this shrine to sorcery and black magic.

**Thackray Medical Museum**
**Leeds, West Yorkshire, England**

Visit a museum that's alive with history—and horrors.

**The British Museum**
**London, England**

Discover a cursed coffin.

**The Louvre**
**Paris, France**

Could this be the most haunted place in Paris?

**Queen's House, National Maritime Museum**
**Greenwich, England**

Spirits linger on spiraling stairs at this royal home.

Arctic Ocean

EUROPE

ASIA

AFRICA

Indian Ocean

AUSTRALIA

Southern Ocean

ANTARCTICA

# Glossary

**afflict** (uh-FLIKT) to cause pain or harm to someone else

**anesthesia** (an-uhs-THEE-zhuh) a drug given to people to put them to sleep and prevent them from feeling any pain

**artifacts** (ART-uh-fakts) objects of historical interest made by people

**casts** (KASTS) objects made by shaping liquid materials in molds

**clairvoyant** (klair-VOI-uhnt) a person who is able to communicate with dead people

**conjoined** (kuhn-JOIND) stuck together

**curiosities** (kyoo-ree-OS-i-teez) things that are unusual and interesting

**dead ringer** (DED RING-er) a person or thing that closely resembles another

**executed** (EK-suh-kyoo-tid) put to death

**extinct** (ek-STINGKT) no longer existing

**folklore** (FOHK-lor) the traditional beliefs, stories, and customs of a people

**grisly** (GRIZ-lee) causing horror or fear

**massacre** (MAS-uh-ker) the violent killing of many people

**melded** (MELD-ed) became merged or fused together

**mortuary** (MOR-choo-air-ee) a place where dead bodies are kept

**possessed** (puh-ZEST) controlled by a spirit

**potent** (POHT-nt) very strong; powerful

**priestess** (PREE-stis) a woman who leads or performs religious ceremonies

**pulsating** (PUHL-seyt-ing) steadily beating or throbbing

**royal** (ROI-uhl) having to do with or belonging to a king or queen

**saliva** (suh-LYE-vuh) a clear liquid produced in the mouths of humans and many animals

**secluded** (si-KLOO-did) hidden from view; placed apart from other people

**serial killers** (SIHR-ee-uhl KIL-uhrz) people who murder more than one person

**severed** (SEV-uhrd) removed by cutting

**shrine** (SHRINE) a place or object people visit because it's connected with someone important

**shrouded** (SHROUD-ed) hidden by a cloth or other covering

**slaughtered** (SLAW-terd) violently killed

**sorcery** (SAWR-suh-ree) the use of magical powers

**summon** (SUHM-uhn) to order someone or something to appear

**surgeon** (SUR-juhn) a doctor who performs operations

**tendons** (TEN-duhnz) strong cords that join muscles to bones

**tumors** (TOO-muhrz) unusual lumps or growths in the body

# Bibliography

**Austin, Joanne.** *Weird Hauntings: True Tales of Ghostly Places.* New York: Sterling (2006).

**Pietras, David.** *America's 100 Most Haunted Locations.* New York: CreateSpace Independent Publishing Platform (2015).

# Read More

**Hamilton, John.** *Haunted Places (The World of Horror).* Edina, MN: ABDO (2007).

**Markovics, Joyce.** *Haunted Gotham (Scary Places).* New York: Bearport (2017).

**Williams, Dinah.** *Dark Mansions (Scary Places).* New York: Bearport (2012).

# Learn More Online

To learn more about spooky museums, visit
**www.bearportpublishing.com/ScaryPlaces**

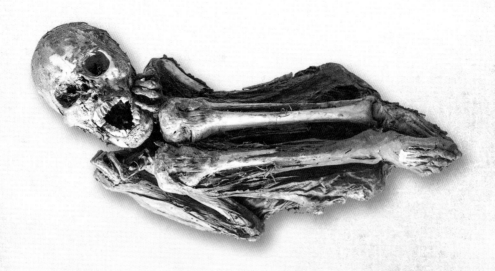

# Index

# About the Author

Joyce Markovics lives in a very, very old house that may
or may not be haunted. She volunteers for Ossining Historic
Cemeteries Conservancy, a group that carefully cleans
and restores historic gravestones.